D0238969

WHERE'S THE MOON,

THERE'S THE MOON

LIS - LIBRARY

Date 25/5	Fund A.e H
Order No. Donation	
University of Chester	

811.
6
CHI

DAN CHIASSON was born in Burlington, Vermont, and educated at Amherst College and Harvard University, where he completed a PhD in English. A widely published literary critic, Chiasson is a regular reviewer for *The New Yorker* and *The New York Times Book Review*, poetry editor of the *Paris Review*, and has published a critical study, *One Kind of Everything: Poem and Person in Contemporary America*, with the University of Chicago Press in 2007.

His Bloodaxe selection *Natural History and other poems* (2006) drew on two collections published in the US, *The Afterlife of Objects* (University of Chicago Press, 2002) and *Natural History* (Alfred A. Knopf, 2005). His latest collection is *Where's the Moon, There's the Moon* (Alfred A. Knopf, US / Bloodaxe Books, UK, 2010). Both of his Bloodaxe titles are Poetry Book Society Recommendations.

He has received a Guggenheim Fellowship for poetry, a Pushcart Prize and a Whiting Writers' Award, and teaches at Wellesley College. He lives in Sudbury, Massachusetts.

DAN CHIASSON

WHERE'S THE MOON, THERE'S THE MOON

BLOODAXE BOOKS

Copyright © Dan Chiasson 2010

ISBN: 978 1 85224 871 0

This edition published 2010 by
Bloodaxe Books Ltd,
Highgreen,
Tarset,
Northumberland NE48 1RP.

First published in the USA in 2010 by Alfred A. Knopf.

www.bloodaxebooks.com
For further information about Bloodaxe titles
please visit our website or write to
the above address for a catalogue.

Supported by
**ARTS COUNCIL
ENGLAND**

LEGAL NOTICE
All rights reserved. No part of this book may be
reproduced, stored in a retrieval system, or
transmitted in any form, or by any means, electronic,
mechanical, photocopying, recording or otherwise,
without prior written permission from Bloodaxe Books Ltd.

Requests to publish work from this book must be
sent to Bloodaxe Books Ltd.

Dan Chiasson has asserted his right under
Section 77 of the Copyright, Designs and Patents Act 1988
to be identified as the author of this work.

Typesetting: North Market Street Graphics, Lancaster, Pensylvania

Book design: Soonyoung Kwon

Cover design: Neil Astley & Pamela Robertson-Pearce

Printed in Great Britain by
Bell & Bain Limited, Glasgow, Scotland.

for Louis and Nicholas

ACKNOWLEDGMENTS

These poems were written with support from the American Academy of Arts and Letters, the John Simon Guggenheim Memorial Foundation, the Whiting Foundation, and Wellesley College. Special thanks to my colleagues in the English Department at Wellesley College.

Poems from this book appeared first in the following publications: *The New Yorker* ("Mosaic of a Hare," "Corinium, 100 AD," "Man and Derailment," "Lincoln's Dream," "Needle's Eye," "Thread"), *The Paris Review* ("Here Follows an Account of the Nature of Birds," "Roman Song," "Where's the Moon, There's the Moon: A Story for Children"), *Ploughshares* ("Etruscan Song"), *Slate* ("Swifts," except for "Thread" and "Needle's Eye"), *The Believer* ("Orbit," "Next," "Hide and Seek," "Stadium," "Herbarium II"), *Southwest Review* ("Blake," "Bluet"). "Lincoln's Dream" was featured in *Jason Dodge* (Editions Yvon Lambert, Paris).

Thanks to my editor, Deborah Garrison; to my wife, Annie Adams; and to Frank Bidart and Louise Glück. This book is dedicated to my children, Louis and Nicholas Chiasson.

CONTENTS

I. SWIFTS

II. WHERE'S THE MOON, THERE'S THE MOON

A Story for Children   37

III: CODA: HIDE-AND-SEEK

I.

SWIFTS

Here Follows an Account of the Nature of Birds

Here Follows an Account of the Nature of Fish.
Here follows a description of an unknown town.
Here follows the phoenix-flight from human eyes.
Here follow the friendship fish and langouste.
All the marvels of erotic danger follow here.
Here follows the phone number of a dead person.
Here follows a game based on perfect information.
Here follows the address of a place to buy cocaine.
Big sadness come your way, sunrise, skyline.
Let's do it some new way next time we try.
Do you have anything you can put inside me?
Here Follows an Account of the Nature of Birds.

Aquarium

I am full of secrets, but none of them is yours.
You can't confide in the outside world.
The surface of the glass is your only conceivable body.

These traces of movement, sudden shadows, they're not fish.
There are varieties of life unknown to you.
Their whole identity is: you can't find out.

You can't find out, however hard you try, no matter
what you say, however "advanced" you are:
they swim away, these things that are not fish.

Look at those bodies on the street. Do you see
how beautifully designed the human body is?
How can you compare your column for containing water?

My mind contains everything except for fish.
The rumor of depth is your new atmosphere.
You can't confide in me. I'm not an aquarium.

Mosaic of a Hare, Corinium, 100 AD

The boats pulling in, the boats pulling out, the top-hat
commerce of the "infant century," crowds, crowds,
"the certainty of others," the bomb
that filled the air with horsehair and the ambulance after:

why wouldn't I hide in my little glass body? I have a clover-sprig
made of glass to aspire to, with my glass appetite.
I raise certain questions about art and its relation to stasis,
yet I despise the formalists as naïve and ahistorical.

Here's my problem with America: this "would be" that
    obliterates
all other moods, playing over and over in people's heads,
the abstract optative that destiny works out.
I don't have the luxury to think in terms of destiny.

What nobody seems to get about me is, though you're made
    of glass
it doesn't mean you don't have appetites: I do. Or fears: I do.
The day the darkness took the whole basilica, I was afraid;
and equally afraid the day, centuries later, they switched
    the lights on.

Let rabbits think in terms of destiny: Whitman, the great
American rabbit poet, the rabbits in the government,
the rabbits that light and the ones that snuff out the fuse,
and all their pretty rabbit children, waiting to be casserole.

Swifts

It is impossible for me to remember
the cozy room I slept in as a child.
Somebody made my bed up to be paradise.
It was hard for me, a hard night, when I entered art.

The tendons in my wrist are visible.
What will I do now I have made this fist?
To loosen it feels weird, anticlimactic—
a misuse, a misunderstanding, of fists.

That's how it was with me that night.
And so, mysteriously, I lost my sweetness.
Weird, to feel intended for violence,
when what I wanted was an hour of rest.

2. THREAD

I lack the rigor of a lightning bolt,
the weight of an anchor. I am
frayed where it would be highly useful—
and this I feel perpetually—to make a point.

I think if I can concentrate I might turn sharp.
Only, I don't know how to concentrate—
I know the look of someone concentrating,
indistinguishable from nearsightedness.

It is hard for the others to be near me,
my silly intensity shuffling
a zillion insignia of interiority.
Being near me never made anyone a needle.

for Jason Dodge

3. WIND

Find some other reason to sway, forest;
old people get bent over
from vitamin deficiencies; trees,
take them as your inspiration.

For I have neither time nor energy
any longer to write poems, to make feeling
out of what, without me, is silent;
I find your standing there disgusting.

And you, reader, I see you nod your head,
treelike, appraising these lines;
I find your standing there—
not disgusting, but not inspiring either.

4. TREE

All day I waited to be blown;
then someone cut me down.

I have, instead of thoughts,
uses; uses instead of feelings.

One day I'll feel the wind again.
A moment later I'll be gone.

5. CAUSE

Whitman wrote this, before he started writing poetry.
He was a journalist for years, you know;
a radical, a partisan for some ridiculous cause.

He wrote this to support—or was it to condemn?—a cause.
It doesn't matter if you aren't Whitman yet.
Now that he's been Whitman for so long, it would.

6. EFFECT

Everything scatters as the night wears on:
but you, don't scatter, will you?
I think we could make this night last forever.

With our joined heads, like mathematicians,
we could work all night, so that
where night once was, work would be; and night,

as long as work went on, would never end.
It is starting to sound a little tiring:
all this working, just to stave off morning.

7. NEEDLE'S EYE

I wish I were as big as a basketball hoop.
It is actually painful to be this fine.
It is like squinting for no reason,
all night, choosing the pain of squinting
over going to sleep. And yet,
what does it matter how big
a target you are? Someone somewhere
will invent a game to make you hard to hit.

8. SOUND, 2 A.M.

A minute ago I was a child coughing: having had
too much of everything today, except for air.

Now I am an animal, feeling, tonight, perplexed—
I fled the outside, the cold, the lack of food;

I meant to enter a house, which I connect with warmth,
which my body told me was the appropriate move.

Instead I entered a person's mind. Like the child,
I am trapped: I have no will, no life to call my own.

9. SWIFTS

Reality isn't one point in space.
It isn't one moment in time—
look at time, a spool of twine
one minute, idle in a sewing kit,
the next minute a shooting star.

Reality is an average of moods,
strike that, a flock of birds,
strike that, a single bird
tracked through dense forest:

you can lose it for hours or days,
but it isn't lost. You tired of the metaphor.

10. CARESS

The tendons flattened and the knot untied.
You could do anything, then, with your hand;
you could forget the fact you had a hand.
This lasted, or so you were tempted to think,
for years; winter didn't matter,
yet spring arrived as a blessing to your body.
Sweetness, or what passed for it, returned;
and then, like an anchor yanked suddenly
from the sea, your muscles clenched.

Roman Song

Shit is the taste you want in your mouth,
sayeth Love, sayeth Love, *You be a dog,*
I lost my heart in the gutter, in the filth,
carry it back to me in your teeth.

Sayeth Love, *You be a dog,* find the butcher
and the gutter, the runoff,
the blood stream flooding the sewer:
the water that sickens quenches desire.

Nothing breathing escapes your appetite.
Nothing to drink is an alien thirst.
Put everything living down your throat.
Your belly is as vast as the world tonight.

Ignore your master's leash. Let food
be your master. Let everything
be food. Let everything taste good.
Let everything you eat be your good food.

A Posy

The cocklebur and ergot, horse chestnut, fescue taste not,
neither taste the green false hellebore nor jimsonweed
nor larkspur, nor even the wild black cherry, pigweed,
pokeweed, lupine and Easter lily; regarding the cherry
there is a story, there is a story regarding the fescue,
men tell a tale about the green false hellebore, there are
accounts of the cherry, pokeweed, the jack-in-the-pulpit:
taste not, lest your skin harden, tingling like cooled wax;
lest your muscles straighten and snap like a candle
taste not the red oak lest your eyes redden and swell—

if you are hungry in this world you are in grave peril,
if it is food you want in this world beware, take care
never to go hungry so that the cocklebur or ergot say
jimsonweed pokeweed say *I am bread* lupine say *I am bread*

"When Spring Opens . . ."

When spring opens the faucet out pours water, water;
if there were a baby playing in the driveway it would be
carried away, water would carry away every baby like the movie
based on a novel based on real life where the school bus
free-falls off the sheer rock cliff. Here is what to do
with the water: find a fire somewhere and put out the fire.
Here is what to do: imagine the desert, nothing stretching
on all sides. Here is what to do: build a boat, find
a mountaintop. Here: turn yourself into a tropical fish.

Or should we plant, which is always to say, should we
have planted: last season, last fall, handfuls of bulbs,
a tree peony or Russian sage; and if we should have planted
what will we do now, spring is here, someone turned on
the spring faucet, a crocus opens across the street, but
we are barren? What to plant. What to have planted.
Yes absolutely there is someone you can call to come over,
have a look at your calendar, and plant when you should have
what you should have planted. Only problem is, you're in

a pornographic film. You have to let him fuck you first
with a contract and a gardening smock. But tulips
and daffodils and lilies will help you keep the summer
ever after. It is a bargain many a man ends up making.

When the nights turned cold, when it turned night early,
we should have planted. Imagine how happy we would be now
if, rather than attending the seminar, I'd taken the bulbs
from the drawer and scattered them everywhere. We would have
flowers in this order: crocus, daffodil, tulip, lily.

Etruscan Song

No love like mine; no love
transformed a hotel room into a womb
and a womb into the child's cry;
no love, no love, no love like mine.

Read in the dark, one hand on dick
Etruscan lore in my Etruscan book—
justice had another flavor there,
buried the son to punish the father.

Drove down the Merritt Parkway
one night, alone, singing *please bury me;*
drove up the following afternoon
with a spade saying *dig me up, someone;*

dug up, found the sun so hot it burned;
craved the chocolate cool of dirt,
the pupa-life underground,
the coffin-dark of a dirt coffin.

So made, no love like mine, a boy;
turned dirt from chocolate to clay;
the clay became, one day, a cry,
and the cry turned night to day.

Monitor

The device that broadcast my heart now broadcasts static.
If you want happiness, that's another animal.
Each animal conveys a single, unwavering emotion.
If you surround yourself with sadness, you seem happy.
Empty repetition is the fruit of the soul.
If it's pretty, that means it wants its face maimed.
Things with hearts and things without are not different.
Any round object is as good as an eye and can see.
The heart of the quiet boy is as dumb as a toy drum.
The lion is empathetic. The crow's belly is full.
The cow is credulous prey. What happened to the horse.
Take any toy you like away from the quiet boy.

Man and Derailment

When the man took his son down the ravine
to view, along the opposite bank,
the pileup of a passenger train,
backhoes and cranes, things the child had seen
only in miniature, now huge, hauling
life-size train cars out of the deep ravine,
inside his life-size head the quiet boy
wondered how he would remember the scene
and, once he knew his father better, later,
and later, knew himself better, what it would mean.

Skylab

You don't lose your identity when you turn lonely.
Your identity deepens, like quicksand.
Parked in orbit, you await another astronaut.

Think of the butterfly: solitary, taken and blown
by a gust of wind, nevertheless he is busy
perfecting the precise terms of his identity.

Ask D.W. Winnicott, if you're so keen to know
why they hung you in space to rot, before
they scattered your body all over the planet.

Satellites

I. BANQUETTE

The satellite that crisscrossed the sky
one day encountered gravity—
the moment it hit the water
it was in a different documentary.

So why would I give it a thought
what you do all night in your apartment
when you're mine on the street
and mine, now, in this suede banquette?

2. BULLET

What counts as a target and what does not
is not innate or inevitable.
One minute your eye falls limply
like a net. The next it becomes a bullet.

What counts as a bullet follows the same rule:
inert, a lump of something small,
chalky in the palm of your hand,
finds its fate (it has a fate) when it gets shot.

3. NIGHT SCENE

Meanwhile, standing by: the stars;
a field where the moon shines;
clouds suddenly darken the field.
If nothingness were a rug, we'd buy it.

Houses go uncharted, week after week;
whole lifetimes happen on schedule,
a child arrives without incident,
grows up to be an astronaut I mean assassin.

4. ORBIT

You have this big capacity, small speck:
barely there at all until
the sun detects your metal shell,
then only a pinprick;

and yet you can predict the moment,
having already lived it,
lived through it, laughed it off,
we thought our child would suffer forever.

5. NEXT

If you can orbit the planet, why can't you see
what makes the human heart happy?
Is it art or is it sex?
Or is it, as I suspect, just keeping going

from next thing to next thing
to next thing to next thing
to next to next to next to next
pulsating stupidly to outlast time?

6. COLERIDGE

"The inmates of my cottage, all at rest":
abstruse my ass, I want a sandwich.
The body is Conan the Barbarian.
Night walk and the sky is gigantic,

but not as lofty as its reputation,
just as I, Mr Friendless and Unloyal,
Conan the Nobody's Around,
now attempt to wash down lead with acid.

Flowers have faces. They are happy or sad.
Their faces change, like ours;
unlike us, it doesn't mean
uh-oh a new mood out of nowhere dawned.

Technically it is immoral to kill a flower
but people do it all the time,
to smooth something over or to please a lover.
Nature just rolls right on, headless.

8. ABSTRUSER MUSINGS

To be no one at all, merely the latest
to have had his brain
turned inside out by vanity,
so that it shine entirely on itself—

is this what M.H. Abrams called "the lamp"?
I call it masturbation,
not as an insult but an accurate name:
it feels good doing it, and people like to watch.

9. BLAKE

A satellite sees into your heart.
It is blind to the rest of the planet.
Its giant eye stares all day
at the one bull's-eye on its one target.

It sees that your heart is sick. You're sick.
All that it sees is the fact
your heart, that once held endless joy,
now sick, soon will "thy life destroy."

LIBRARY UNIVERSITY OF CHESTER

Lincoln's Dream

It is impossible to state just how in love I am
with my own body, the white snows of me,
the sudden involutions and crevasses of me,
my muscles tensed or slack in anger or fear.

This is why, wherever I am, I am in Lincoln's dream.
A sentry stands by, the stairway is eerily lit,
light is a little milk-stain on people's faces,
the faces of my cabinet, grotesque and funny masks.

Who is dead in the White House? I demand. *Who's not?*
answers a soldier, pointing to a shrouded head
on my own body, encased like a gangly insect
on the catafalque, and the loud wails wake me up.

Reader, when you caress yourself in the morning,
amazed that you are made the way you are,
sure that yours is the finest body of all,
remember, you are Lincoln having Lincoln's dream.

Train

You there, in the middle of your mind,
curled up into a ball but wide awake—
I am awake like you, in the same bed

hearing the train that when it passes
means it's almost morning, though the sky
is dark, though the highway is quiet.

You can follow the train in your mind,
but your mind cannot follow the train
from little town to little town to Boston

where in the dark the transactions happen—
something is poured, something is filled,
something is dropped off, something is taken—

happen among the loud men at the wharf
before their very first sign of dawn,
and the train in Boston turns around.

I wish our minds were like the train,
passing once a night through the woods,
fading out among the lights and termini,

its load of oil or metal going someplace
they want it, returning in the morning,
its mile-long belly not empty, not hungry;

not the wharf, accepting train after train
of junk from the provinces all night,
a throat that tries to swallow dirt.

II.

WHERE'S THE MOON,
THERE'S THE MOON

A Story for Children

1.

If I look to the opposite shore and greet myself there,
if I call out to myself *come here*
and watch myself laboriously construct from shore-things
a boat, and watch myself over the waters come rowing,
but, crossing the midpoint between shores,
out in the middle of the colorless lake,
no longer approaching, no longer coming closer,
disappear, where am I now, has my boat capsized?

2.

Infinite capacity for love in the smallest detail;
infinite suffering in the innermost reality;
large mind in even the dumbest, mutest object;
destiny in an object that stands still;
heart in the middle of the grey, motionless water;
the largest sadness in the world in a groaning buoy;
in a buoy and the bird overhead, huge sadness,
and yet I hop from place to place as though I'm weightless.

3.

When I picture my father I see the surface of the moon,
plains of moon-stuff, chalk-dust papers shredded
by a paper-shredder, snowbanks of shredded paper,
nobody to organize it all, no way to "moralize the day
out of its aimlessness," nobody with a Shop-Vac handy
slowly to turn the whiteness into pattern and form,
revealing, as a chisel reveals in the marble,
a figure, a woman's figure, an expression of bliss—

4.

Now that that big nonentity the moon is in my mind
the clichés for representing earth are hereby banished—
a hundred open-ended poems, abrupt transitions, high tones
grating against the low, unsorted experience;
sex beside the holy man defiled by sex,
the pig pile of ways you can get high, right there
beside the dawn and how you badly want to kill yourself,
the fleer, the road that unravels like a banner before him—

5.

And the child's attention fixed upon the animal book,
and all the animals in the book intent upon dinner
or eyeing some harbinger cloud forever, permanently
dejected because some little stone turned their child
to stone, weeping big mule or owl tears as though
the child never turned the page, the sun never shone
again bringing larkspurs, gentian, and the mule-boy
reunited with mule mommy and daddy just in time to end,

6.

but the mule on page four will always be sad, the owl
overhead will always mourn for the mule in his sadness,
nobody will ever bring news of page eleven when mule-boy
returns from the dead, and the child reading the book
will always preside like a sinister god over these animals,
always dipping in and out of their moods like a snacker,
a little sadness to tide you over until suppertime,
a little elegiac owl, some time at the grief picnic . . .

7.

He has lived on the moon for now thirty years,
part of an old guild, virtually a decoration,
but I am proud of him, as was his master-keeper proud
of him, this noble, endless line of moonkeepers
who hang the light that lights the moon and take it down
every morning, meaning that it is morning, get up,
that's not a pie-plate over there in the east,
sleepyheads, lovers climb down off of your beloveds;

8.

as the child is to the book, a watcher, a dabbler
so he is, I think, to my own life, that he may know
or not (his being, in the sky, in a position
that looked at in a certain light affords omniscience
but looked at in another light is blindness pure);
but since he lights and snuffs the lantern
on the moon, I have the illusion of his being nearby,
not in the photonegative of life, snowbanks and cold,

9.

no flowers ever, hardly a bird, nobody to say to you,
want a lick of this? Or here, I have an extra one,
or you can take more and nothing bad will happen,
or I like it a little more than that, or send me,
won't you, one of your new poems, I'd like to have that,
and never the whispered request there, tha-a-a-a-at's it,
r-r-r-right there, and so why would I go to the anti-earth,
not that he asked, but if he did, why would I ever go

10.

stay with him on that windswept sand-planet,
a house here, a house there, no tree, no sod, nothing
not buried in sand, a few moon-plums and moon-peas
the city people gather and preserve in ceramic jars,
and schooners come from Boston to gather the sand
for masonry suppliers back in the city, but sand
sweeps in and fills the deep furrows their shovels leave
and the ugly moon-jays buzz above like house-flies;

11.

and here is the page where the man, the son
of the man who keeps the moon, has fallen asleep;
we are to understand those words he spoke just now
as things said on the verge of sleep, and where,
under the illustration of this man, his words were
there is now only the letter "z" repeated eleven times;
now look, what are those toys and books, what is
that little bed, that moon-mobile above the bed;

12.

and now we turn the page the background changes; the man
is now a boy; he is asleep on the lip of a crater; stars,
real stars, replace the paper-stars of his mobile;
though we resist the easy transformation from man to child,
nevertheless something in the picture is poignant;
this small act of turning the page has changed a person,
he has forgotten, since he is sleeping and he is a child,
the very existence of hard-up, rummaged bathroom stalls;

13.

what could be more beautiful than this, thinks the boy;
I've lost the earth entirely, my head is no longer dense
with somebody else's voice speaking through me
like a sock puppet or large-size microphone contraption,
now my mind is as serene and empty as the moon's surface;
when I open my mouth to speak no sound comes out;
I am like a home movie from the 1960s, vividly alive but
quiet, since the right technology hasn't been invented yet;

14.

bear with me while I try to convey what I want to convey:
my father's distance and yet the tendency of distant things
to become central; my tidelike ups and downs, up-downs
and down-ups and the influence of a superstellar body
upon me; my "poetry" as I hazard to call these writings;
bear with me because this movie, though vividly a record
of somebody saying something, has no sound of its own,
which means I might as well not have a mouth.

15.

Man-boy on his inner journey meets his father
distant, perhaps an artist, perhaps just an asshole,
climbing a ladder to the lamppost where the moon hangs;
looks up in pride to see his father, artist or asshole,
so absorbed in a task, so evidently free and confident,
not sitting around looking bored at his son's every move,
really himself, like an acrobat in mid-somersault,
who wouldn't admire an acrobat-artist doing his thing?

16.

Beauty cannot be gainsaid no matter how sarcastic we are:
the osier braided into a basket used to carry fish,
the fish surrounded by ripe plums on a wooden platter;
the knife gleaming as we see the flesh of the fish
tugged effortlessly apart from the fish's spine;
the spoonful of honeyed water with which to dress
the small piece of fish in the middle of our white plate;
wine in a glass, the person next to us gossiping;

17.

or this: "Two men in a skiff, whom we passed hereabouts,
floating buoyantly amid the reflections of the trees, like
a feather in mid air, or a leaf which is wafted gently
from its twig to the water without turning over,
seemed still in their element, and to have very delicately
availed themselves of the natural laws. Their floating
served to ennoble in our eyes the art of navigation, for
as birds fly and fishes swim, so these men sailed."

18.

Or this: "If there is nothing new on the earth, still
the traveller always has a new resource in the skies.
They are constantly turning a new page to view.
The wind sets the types on this blue ground, and
the inquiring may always read a new truth there.
There are things there written with such fine
and subtil tinctures, paler than the juice of limes . . .
only the chemistry of night reveals them."

19.

The winterberry by the road is not red at midnight.
Everyone dies every night and wakes up a new person.
If you want a mystery, study what you did yesterday.
My genome has its own ideas in store for me.
A cloud covered the heavens and now the constellation
archer, target, isn't visible at all. These metaphors
add up to one conclusion: I own a thirsty horse
and yet I use his trough as our centerpiece.

20.

In our inattention, the child has come close to finishing
The Moonkeeper's Son, and learned how a grown man yearns
to go back to his time, beside his father, on the moon,
and dreams he is back there in childhood, which is
a kind of moon (this point the author intends), though mine
had a lot more pewter figurines of Christ strewn around it
than the moon, at least as it is classically represented,
would; a kind of moon, and fathers come and go, don't they,

21.

the way the moon waxes and wanes (the author intends this)
but what the author does not intend is the following point:
the moon orbits the earth; it heads out in a straight line
but despite itself, despite its best attempts, cants
a little (feel it?) to the right, like a boat without
the starboard oar, and soon its straight-line ambitions
pass the point where they began, as indeed they must
if counteracted by a force designed to keep them close.

22.

The fact of it, the fact that such a force exists:
that is the force. Your straight line loops back
and over and over the comedy of your life would be
the flight, the return, the child sitting in the middle
lassoing you through orbit, over and over; this lesson
is not the author's intention, nor is it mine;
but my intentions cannot be taken into account in this case
since I am a sketch on paper of a person speaking,

23.

lines drawn to resemble a person age 36 years, 3 months,
name Chiasson, Dan, mind tracked in real time
by a satellite whose sophisticated gauges measure
not merely geologic disturbances in the earth's surface
but also, it must be granted, meaning, as in what
did I mean by "lasso" back there or why in the world
in a poem about my childhood would I include
these stray, albeit gorgeous, perceptions of Thoreau?

24.

We're all of us central; we're all of us the subject
of interstellar scrutiny; everybody's readout shows
a small volcano astraddle the middle of middle island;
you're tracked by this satellite that sees the faults
that crack the crust and cause the coup; you have two eyes,
don't you? You own two hands that hold the pages close
to see what's written even "in fine and subtil tinctures"?
Would you describe this as a prison or a country club?

25.

This mouth is being erased before your eyes. Goodbye.
These eyes are being erased before your eyes. Goodbye.
No chin anymore. No nose anymore. These cheeks are gone.
The outline of my head, my wild Dan white-man Afro, gone.
Without a head you do not have a mind. Without a mind
even the little confidences, sotto voce, dry up.
Now the eraser passes over my limbs, and now
the ground I rested on, the cartoon tree, all gone.

26. "Hide Thy Life"

Hide Thy Life, sayeth the tablet, Hide Thy life;
mind not the robin in the buddleia;
mind not the forsythia aflame;
mind not the first bloodroot,
the mayflower, mind not;
you are the single phony thing
outdoors today; where did you find that mind?
Put that mind right back where you found it.

27.

Sweet-hearted mules, living in a village near kind chickens,
constable pigs, an elderly neighbor donkey couple,
mules, it is winter, but quit your weeping, your thrashing
at your shirts, your pacing up and down the floor;
mule-child, your angel, is not dead; on page four
he is changed into a rock, a sketch of a rock;
But lo, I bring the news of page eighteen: there, you three
embrace again, all grief erased. A family: a sketch of joy.

III.

CODA: HIDE-AND-SEEK

LIBRARY, UNIVERSITY OF CHESTER

Herbarium

Jasmine means passion and privet
means private. If they are bound together
in a book, hidden underground, a famous book,

off-limits in a library, which one wins:
privet, that kept the secret,
or jasmine, that made the privet shine?

Stadium

An empty stadium is an indrawn breath.
There hasn't been a team here in ages.
Futuristic is starting to look very old.

It's a vast cereal bowl; and in it,
bobbing like a raisin, there's my childhood.
I'm rooting for the nonexistent team.

Waterfall

Meanwhile like a treadmill a waterfall
pours its entire body
downstream, going nowhere, pours

and is filled by the nothing waters
upstream, as though gravity
needed something to gloat about.

Hide-and-Seek

Once, north of here, a child played
hide-and-seek. His part was to hide,
ergo he played his role and hid.

The seeker, embarrassed by his role,
thinking it beneath his dignity,
developed instead a personality disorder.

Herbarium (II)

Once, west of here, a child fastened
flowers to the pages of a book,
and wrote their names in Latin underneath.

This was the pinnacle of mimesis.
The flowers are so brittle now
nobody is allowed to open that book.

Olympic Stadium, Montreal

There is no name for the tendency
of things to start to fall apart
before they are complete, but

that isn't because the phenomenon
is rare: to the contrary,
little poem: this is the common condition.

Falls, Bristol, VT

The waterfall runs all day and night,
shedding big self on the rocks below,
refilling with more self, more self, more self,

while bathers visit in small groups, never
the same bathers, always the same river—
my local, inverted, redneck pre-Socratic.

Revolving Door

I spit and swallow with equal gusto.
Spitting is not a sign of disgust.
Swallowing is not a sign of hunger.

Casting out is not a sign of anger.
Allowing in is not affection.
I chug along, doing what I'm meant to do.

Hide-and-Seek (II)

Hide and seek, hide and seek: the magic trick
of keeping time in play by yo-yo
mini-episodes of loss and recovery.

One day that game goes dark, and you want
a new game whose object isn't loss.
The rule is: everyone stay close by, in sight.

Previews

It was the newest movie, and we arrived early.
Something bright and loud was playing,
not the movie, but not that different from the movie.

Infinitely elongated Beforehand, bright Not Yet:
our children grew impatient in your zone.
We left the movie before the movie began.

NOTES

The title poem of this book is organized loosely according to William Steig's great children's story, "Sylvester and the Magic Pebble." The quotations from Henry David Thoreau can be found in *A Week on the Concord and Merrimack Rivers*. The phrase "moralize the day out of its aimlessness" is adapted from William Butler Yeats's "Meditations in Time of Civil War."

"Satellites" draws on Samuel Taylor Coleridge's "Frost at Midnight" and William Blake's "The Sick Rose," as well as M.H. Abrams's *The Mirror and the Lamp*.

The herbarium in the poems by that name is Emily Dickinson's, now available in facsimile from Harvard University Press.